MY FIRST BIBLE Coloring Book

This book belongs to:

_____

ANNA
anna s. luce

Thank you so much for choosing

MY FIRST BIBLE COLORING BOOK

for toddlers and kids ages 2+

Help your toddler get acquainted with the main stories of the Bible as well as with some of the most important religious symbols and characters – by coloring <u>60 SIMPLE and BIG Christian illustrations.</u>

Each design also includes the word that describes it, written in hollow letters for easy coloring. As your child colors, help him/her learn these words and understand the meaning of each Christian symbol in a friendly and playful way.

Did you like our book? Please <u>consider dropping us a review</u>. It takes only a few seconds and it really helps small businesses like ours reach more readers. Your support means the world to us!

Check out other book by <u>Anna S. Luce</u> on Amazon!

ADAM AND EVE IN THE GARDEN OF EDEN

JONAH

JONAH SWALLOWED BY A BIG FISH

THE BURNING BUSH

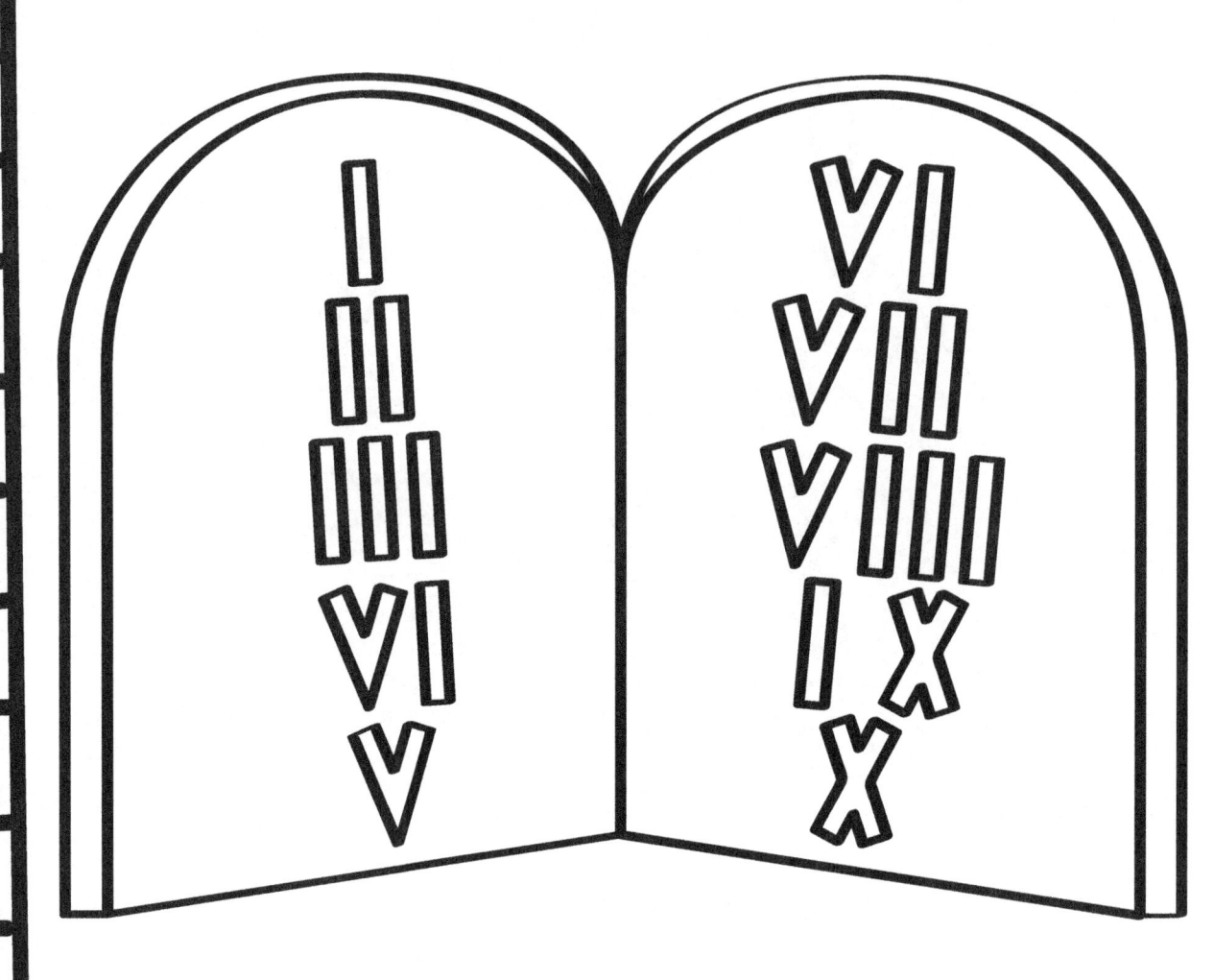

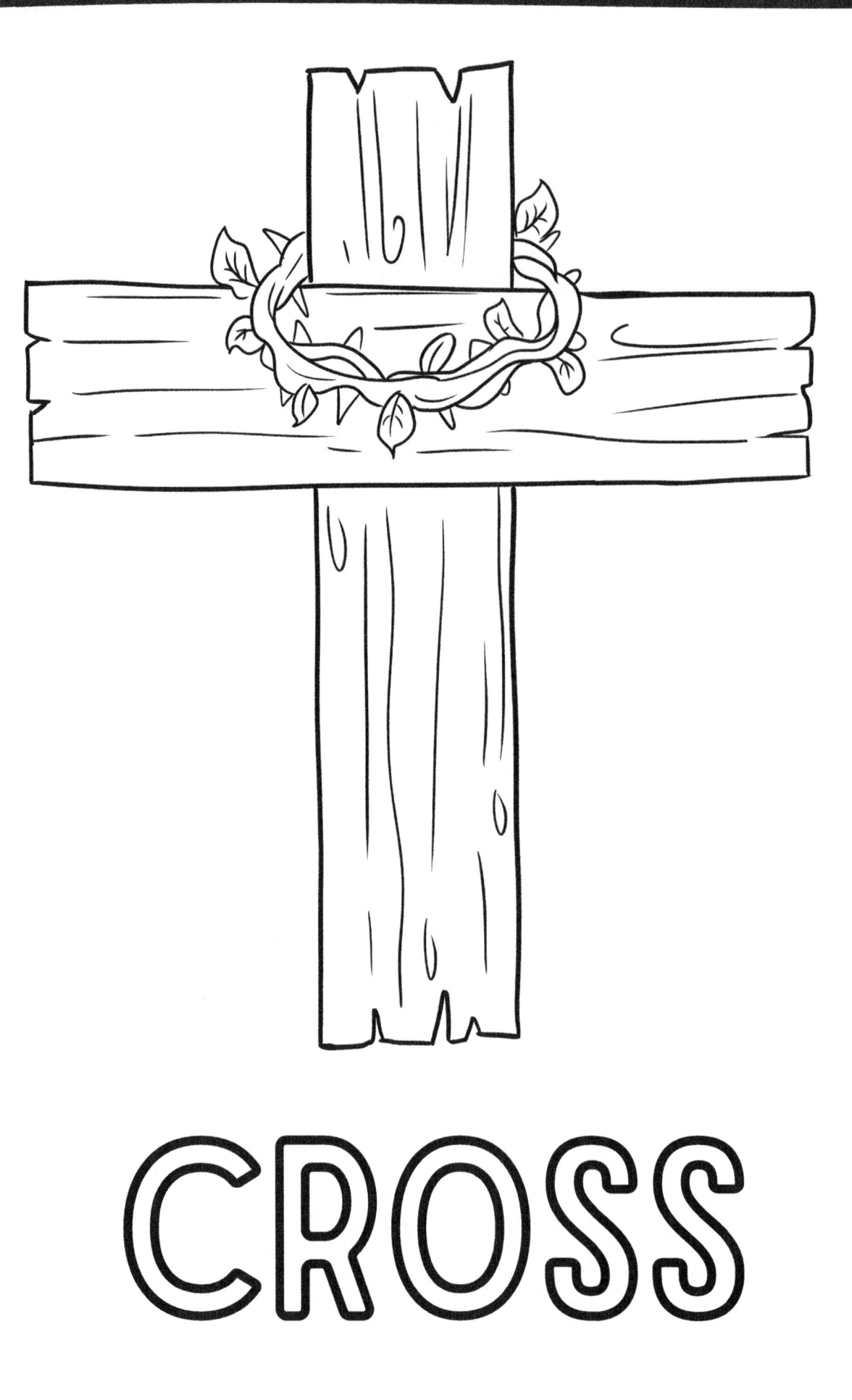

THE EMPTY TOMB

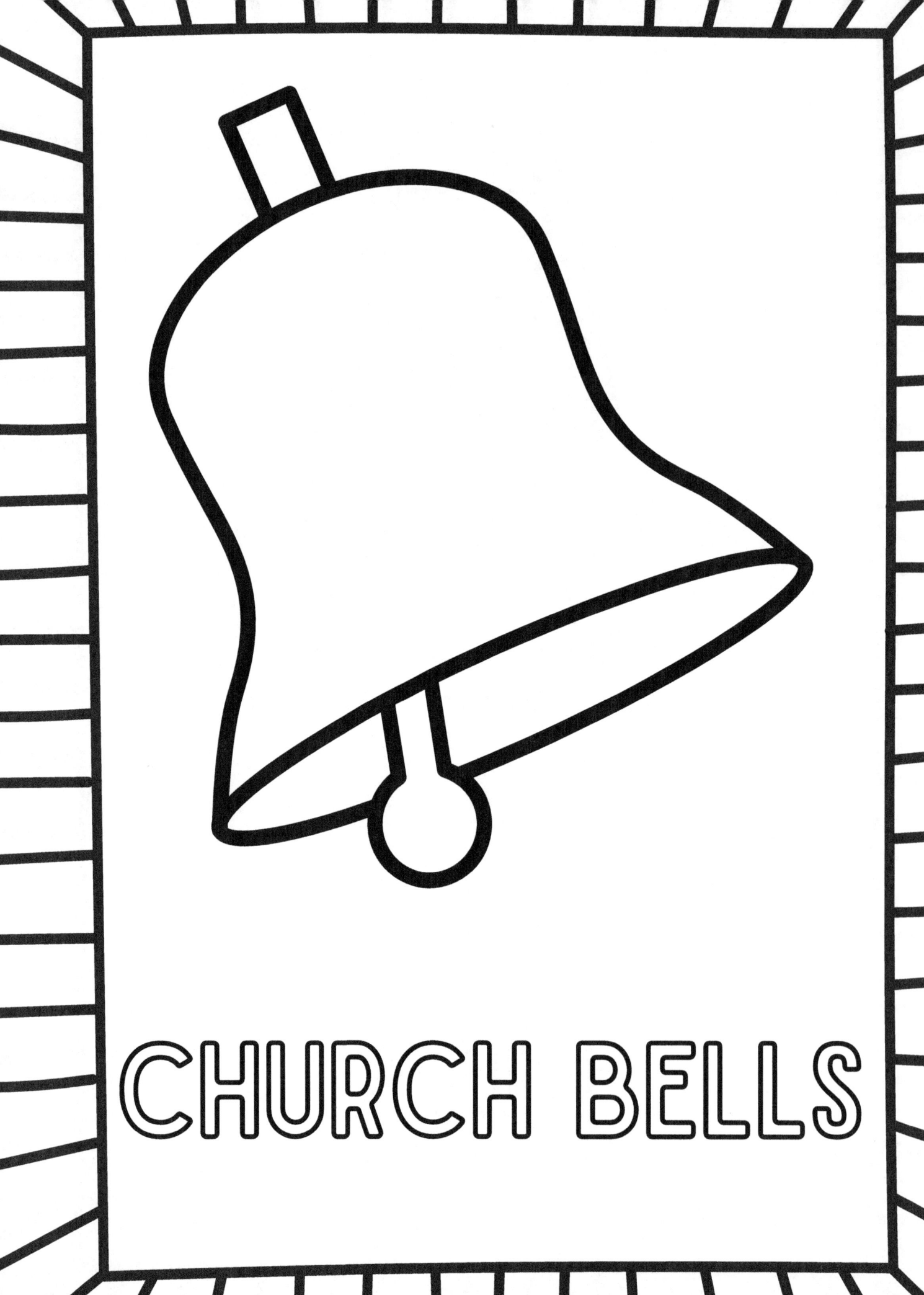

God Bless You

My First Bible Coloring Book
for Toddlers and Kids Ages 2+

© Copyright 2023 - All rights reserved. No part of this publication may be reproduced, distributed, or transmitted in any form or by any means without the prior written permission of the publisher, except as permitted by U.S. copyright law. You can use the book for personal purpose only. Disclaimer: the information in this book is for casual reading and entertainment purposes only.

Printed in Great Britain
by Amazon